SIR WALTER RALEIGH

Sir WALTER RALEGH Knt.
Captain of the Queens Guard Lord Warden
of the Stanneries Lieutenant General of the
AMORE ET

SIR WALTER RALEIGH

BY

HENRY DAVID THOREAU

LATELY DISCOVERED AMONG HIS UNPUBLISHED JOURNALS
AND MANUSCRIPTS

INTRODUCTION BY

FRANKLIN BENJAMIN SANBORN

EDITED BY

HENRY AIKEN METCALF

BOSTON : MDCDV
PRINTED EXCLUSIVELY FOR MEMBERS OF
THE BIBLIOPHILE SOCIETY

What makes a hero? An heroic mind
Express'd in action, in endurance proved:
And if there be pre-eminence of right,
Derived through pain well suffer'd, to the height
Of rank heroic, 'tis to bear unmoved,
Not toil, not risk, not rage of sea or wind,
Not the brute fury of barbarians blind,
But worse, — ingratitude and poisonous darts
Launch'd by the country he had served and loved.

SIR HENRY TAYLOR, *Heroism in the Shade.*

PREFACE

THE discovery of an unpublished essay by Thoreau on Sir Walter Ralegh is an event of great interest in the world of letters, as being the earliest contribution to literature, of decided scholarly value, of its distinguished author. The original manuscript was purchased by Mr. William K. Bixby, of St. Louis, from Mr. Edward H. Russell, of Worcester, Massachusetts, to whom nearly all of the MSS. and *Journals* of Thoreau came by inheritance; and it is to the generosity of its present owner (Mr. Bixby) that the members of The Bibliophile Society are indebted for the privilege of possessing such an exceedingly rare item of Americana.

When mere *fragments* of hitherto unpublished compositions of our foremost American writers are so eagerly sought, it seems strange that a well-rounded work of perhaps the most original of the noteworthy group of Concord (Massachusetts) thinkers should have remained unknown for nearly sixty years. This is a veritable treasure wherewith still further to enrich the bibliography of the publications of our Society.

It may be well here to remark that simultaneously with this volume the Society has issued Thoreau's *Journey West*, the entirely unpublished MS. notes of which were discovered among the author's *Journals*, and purchased by Mr. Bixby at the same time he acquired the *Sir Walter Ralegh*. We are therefore permitted to bring out, as companion pieces, *first editions* of the first inedited important manuscript written by Thoreau, and also this narrative of his Western journey, which preceded his death by only a few months. These two items will doubtless prove to be one of the most important literary "finds" of the season.

We are fortunate, moreover, in having a special Introduction to each of them prepared by Franklin Benjamin Sanborn, the greatest living authority on Thoreau, of whom he was a life-long friend and neighbor.

There are three drafts of the manuscript of *Sir Walter Ralegh*, each one differing in certain respects from the other two, and all of which have been used in the preparation of this volume. The third, and final, draft, in its careful elaboration, and the skilful weaving together of its parts, is a distinct improvement over the first; and there are some indications, even in this last draft, that the author may have had a still further revision in contemplation.

We are so wont only to associate Thoreau with his own immediate world of Nature, that a work like this in which he ventures so far afield, and in which he deals with so much that is stirring, presents him to us in an entirely new light. Perhaps, at first, we may wonder what there was in common between the retiring, home-loving citizen of Concord, and this adventurous knight of "the spacious days of great Elizabeth," which should make Sir Walter Ralegh his favorite character in English history. But we have only to study the career of this sturdy Devonshire worthy to come under the spell of his enduring charm and real manliness; to admire the unswerving loyalty with which he ever served his country; and to feel, with Robert Louis Stevenson, that "God has made nobler heroes, but He never made a finer gentleman than Walter Ralegh."

To every patriotic American this heroic figure should appeal with a special enthusiasm, since, as Charles Kingsley has said,—"To this one man, under the Providence of Almighty God, the whole United States of America owe their existence."

HENRY AIKEN METCALF

INTRODUCTION

BY

FRANKLIN BENJAMIN SANBORN

THE finding of a sketch of Sir Walter Ralegh (as he usually spelt his own name) among the manuscripts of Thoreau will be a surprise to most readers. But the subject lay along the lines of his earlier readings after leaving Harvard College, and the sketch, though not so early among his writings as *The Service*, edited by me in 1902, and those parts of *The Week* that first came out in *The Dial* (1840–44), belongs in that active and militant period of his life. It was probably prepared for publication in *The Dial*, and would have been published there, had not fate and the lack of paying subscribers abruptly stopped that quarterly in the summer of 1844.

The readings from Ralegh's *History of the World* began about 1842, as we see by the earlier *Journals*, and the handwriting and some other circumstances about the three drafts of the sketch fix the date as not later than 1844. His poetical scrap-book, into which he copied most of those verses of Ralegh's and Ben Jonson s time that appear in *The Week*, along with many others, and which Ellery Channing had before him in writing his *Thoreau the Poet-Naturalist*, opens with three pages copied from the works of Ralegh, and contains in its pages, 130–142, the poetic pieces ascribed to Ralegh in this sketch. It was this commonplace book that Thoreau used in preparing his *Week* for the press in 1848–49, and nothing appears there of later date. The last extracts therein which can be certainly dated are from the *Massachusetts Quarterly Review* of September, 1848, on Hindoo Philosophy. The paging of the book in pencil is later, and so is a list of pages which shows what therein Thoreau had used in his papers for printing. The long passages about Alexander and Epaminondas are in the scrap-book at pages 236–7; and that fine passage about the starry influences stands in the scrap-book on page 235, and in the list of used pages is crossed out. The poem of Du Bartas quoted afterwards does not seem to be in the scrap-book.

Of course, since Thoreau wrote on Ralegh, now more than sixty years, much has been learned and printed concerning his problematical career, which still remains in some points doubtful, — in none more so, perhaps, than in the true authorship of the poems ascribed to him by his contemporaries, and long after by Bishop Percy.

Thoreau seems to have been guided in his judgment of Ralegh as the real author of disputed poems, by his inner consciousness of what the knightly courtier ought to have written. Nor did he live long enough to see the fragments of an undoubted poem by Ralegh, *The Continuation of Cynthia*, which was found after Thoreau's death among the numerous papers of the Cecils at Hatfield House. In its form it is the poorest of all the verses ascribed to Ralegh ; yet it has good lines, and a general air of magnanimous regret. It is a fragment in the unmistakable handwriting of Ralegh, with all his peculiarities of spelling, such as "soon" for sun, "yearth" for earth, "sythes" for sighs, and "perrellike" for pearl-like. The *Cynthia* of which it is a continuation is irrecoverably lost, but was mentioned by Spenser in his *Colin Clout's Come Home Again*, as early as 1593, where he calls Ralegh "the Shepheard of the Ocean," and says, —

> His song was all a lamentable lay
> Of great unkindness and of usage hard,
> Of Cynthia, the Lady of the Sea,
> Which from her presence faultless him debarred.

That, of course, must have been written some time after 1592; the continuation is believed by Archdeacon Hannah to have been written soon after the death of Elizabeth (his Cynthia) and during his own early imprisonment in the Tower. Thoreau's favorite among Ralegh's poems was *The Lie*, or as he preferred to call it, *The Soul's Errand*, which was long disputed as Ralegh's, but is now certainly known to be his, by the direct testimony of two contemporary manuscripts, "and the still stronger evidence," says Hannah, "of at least two contemporary answers, written during his lifetime, and reproaching him with the poem, by name or implication." Thoreau had at first taken it for Ralegh's without doubt; then found, in a newspaper of 1843, a version of it ascribed to Joshua Sylvester, the translator of Du Bartas, which led him to doubt its being Ralegh's, and to alter his version of the text. This later version he read at the Concord funeral of John Brown (December 2, 1859), prefacing it with these words: "The well-known verses called *The Soul's Errand*, supposed by some to have been written by Sir Walter Raleigh, when he was expecting to be executed on the following day, are at least worthy of such an origin, and are equally applicable to the present case. Hear them," — and he proceeded to read them in my hearing. But on a blank page in the scrap-book he wrote in pencil, "Assigned to Raleigh by Percy, as written the night before his execution. But it appeared in *Poetical Rhapsody* in 1608, yet, as Davison says, may have been written the night before he expected to have been executed in 1603. It is found among Sylvester's Poems, and by Ritson given to Davison. It also occurs in Lord Pembroke's Poems, and exists in two copies in the Harleian MSS."

To this comment, written in 1843–44, Archdeacon Hannah added in 1870, "It can be found in MSS. more than ten years earlier than 1608,—in 1596/1595, or 1593. There are five other claimants, but not one with a case that will bear the slightest examination. For the claim of Richard Edwards we are indebted to a mere mistake of Ellis's; for that of F. Davison to a freak of Ritson's; that of Lord Essex is only known from the correspondence of Percy, who did not believe it; and those of Sylvester and Lord Pembroke are sufficiently refuted by the mutilated character of the copies which were printed among their posthumous writings."

Thoreau evidently had his faith in Ralegh's authorship shaken by the attribution to Sylvester in 1843, and the printing then of the extended (rather than mutilated) copy as found in Sylvester, which he proceeded to compare with his earlier copy. As a result, the verses read by him at the

Brown funeral were amended from the Sylvester copy. Hannah has a theory worth citing: "We find grounds for supposing that Ralegh marked each crisis of his history by writing some short poem, in which the vanity of life is proclaimed, under an aspect suited to his circumstances and age. His first slight check occurred in 1589, when he went to visit Spenser in Ireland; and more seriously a little later, when his secret marriage sent him to the Tower. *The Lie*, with its proud, indignant brevity, would then exactly express his angry temper. *The Pilgrimage* belongs more naturally to a time when he was smarting under the rudeness of the king's attorney at his trial in 1603. The few lines, *Even such is Time*, mark the calm reality of the now certain doom; they express the thoughts appropriate for the night now known to be indeed the last, when no room remained for bitterness or anger, in the contemplation of immediate and inevitable death."

I may observe that Thoreau adds a little to the tale of the occasion of these lines in the scrap-book where he copies them.

He writes, "Sir Walter Raleigh the night before his death." (In some copies thus entitled: "Verses said to have been found in his Bible in the Gatehouse at Westminster;" Archbishop Sancroft, who has transcribed the lines, calls them his "Epitaph made by himself, and given to me of him, the night before his suffering.")

The Silent Lover is thought to have been sent to Elizabeth; the Walsingham verses, which Thoreau thought characteristic of Ralegh, do not seem so to me, and Hannah says, "I think it very improbable that Ralegh wrote this ballad." It sounds more like Campion.

As in that chapter of *The Service* which he has called *The Soldier*, so in this essay Thoreau shows a decided taste for war as against an inglorious state of peace, and sees little harm in the constant ardor of his hero for a fight against Irish kernes, Spanish warships, and the armies of Austria and Spain, against which he had contended from his warlike youth, when he absented himself from the university to learn the art of war. Although less inclined, as he grew older, to use the language of campaigns and battle fields, Thoreau never quite gave up this belligerent attitude. He was pugnacious, and rather annoyed by those ostentatious preachers of international peace who mixed themselves in with the anti-slavery and temperance reformers of his period. One such, Henry C. Wright, an aggressive non-resistant, was specially satirized by him in his *Journal* for June 17, 1853,—the anniversary of Bunker Hill battle, and perhaps chosen on that account to make a demonstration against war in Concord, whose chief reputation had once been that it opened the war of the Revolution. It may be mentioned, parenthetically, in passing, that Thoreau's grandmother, Mary Jones of Weston, daughter of the Tory Colonel Jones of the Provincial militia, on the day of Bunker Hill in 1775 came over from Weston to Concord to carry a basket of cherries and other good things to a Tory brother immured in Concord Jail for bringing in supplies from Halifax to the British troops besieged in Boston. She was but a girl, but she soon married Rev. Asa Dunbar, who also was inclined to be a Tory, and did not join the patriots until he went to reside in Keene, N. H., as a lawyer, giving up his clerical profession, since there were few parishes that would tolerate a minister who was not a sincere patriot. Of the Jones family some were Tories and some patriots, the rest, among them Mrs. Dunbar, were neutral. On the contrary, Thoreau's grandfather on the other side was in the Revolutionary service as a privateer.

For whatever reason, this particular peace advocate was not attractive to Thoreau, who thus spoke of him in his *Journal*, as was first noted by Channing in his *Life of Thoreau*; "They addressed each other constantly by their Christian names, and rubbed you continually with the greasy cheek of their kindness. I was awfully pestered with the benignity of one of them. . . . He wrote a book called *A Kiss for a Blow*, and he behaved as if I had given him a blow,—was bent on giving me the kiss, — when there was neither quarrel nor agreement between us. . . . He addressed me as 'Henry' within one minute from the time I first laid eyes on him; and when I spoke he said, with drawling, sultry sympathy, 'Henry, I know all you would say, I understand you perfectly, — you need not explain anything to me.' He could tell in a dark room, with his eyes blinded, and in perfect stillness, if there was one there whom he loved. . . . What a relief to have heard the ring of one healthy, reserved tone." This satirical tone is seldom found in the essay on Ralegh, which, like most of the essays and verses before 1845 are in a serious and often paradoxical spirit, suggesting laughter only by their extravagance, which the young author did not seem to perceive.

The tone of *The Service* was probably suggested by those numerous discourses on peace and non-resistance to which he was obliged to listen from 1840 to 1848, and which he resented then, as he also did in 1859 when writing with some heat on the capture and martyrdom of John Brown, which he compared to that of Ralegh. "I speak for the slave," he said, "when I say that I prefer the philanthropy of Captain Brown to that philanthropy which neither shoots me nor liberates me. For once the Sharp rifles and the revolvers were employed in a righteous cause. I do not wish to kill nor to be killed, but I can foresee circumstances in which both these things would be by me unavoidable." He listened with much interest to Brown's account of his fights in Kansas, when I had introduced him to Brown in his father's house at Concord, in February, 1857, and noted down many of their particulars; and when the Civil War came on, he was as earnest as any one that it should be fought to its just conclusion, the destruction of slavery. In this he was unlike his English friend Thomas Cholmondeley, who wrote to him from Shrewsbury, April 23, 1861: "These rumors of wars make me wish that we had got done with this brutal stupidity of war altogether; and I believe, Thoreau, that the human race will at last get rid of it, though, perhaps, not in a creditable way; but such powers will be brought to bear that it will become monstrous even to the French. Dundonald declared to the last that he possessed secrets which, from their tremendous character, would make war impossible. So peace may be begotten from the machinations of evil."

Lord Dundonald, who had fought by sea for the South Americans and the Greeks, was a good sample of a modern Ralegh; but he would not have aroused in Thoreau the interest which he had felt in Ralegh. It was the literary as well as the knightly quality in the Elizabethan that attracted the Concord man of letters; and the burden of this long-lost essay will be found to be chiefly literary. Ralegh, like his friends, Sidney and Spenser, is one of the romantic figures in English literature more admired than read in these later days; they are indispensable to him who would know all the resources of poesy in our native tongue. I was therefore surprised and rather grieved to hear Dr. Holmes say, as we were returning together to Boston from the breakfast given to Mrs. Stowe at Newton, many years since, that he had never read the verses ascribed to Ralegh. Nobody now reads the *History of the World*, — probably Thoreau was its latest American reader, except those whom some historical task required them to go through with it. He was also the last reader of Davenant's *Gondibert*, upon which many an adventurous youth has been stranded. But Thoreau, like Emerson and Charles Lamb, whose researches in Elizabethan fields aided him, and are acknowledged in his commonplace book, from 1839 until 1845 made a faithful study of that copious and racy literature that filled the century from Surrey and Wyatt to Crashaw and Vaughan, and in this scrap-book before me more than forty authors of that period are quoted, some of them at much length. The editors of Thoreau's dozen volumes should have had this scrap-book before them when seeking the source of the quotations in which he so abounds.

Let us not seek to overvalue this treasure-trove of an author to whom each successive year brings a new army of readers, and of whom every reader becomes a warm admirer. It is not a finished piece of English like many of his essays; he had not in 1844 reached that perfection in his style, nor that ripeness of thought which *Walden* and the later writings display. It belongs, rather, with that collection of literary essays with which the bulk of his narrative of *The Week* is so increased, and its qualities so much enriched. But it shows how early his profound conceptions got a striking expression, and how even earlier his far-reaching judgments on men and things entitled him to the name of scholar and sage.

Few youths of New England ever exhibited sooner in life, or practised more seriously and effectively, the arts and gifts that produce works of permanent literary value. Such is every completed essay of Thoreau that I have seen; and I must now have seen them nearly all. The revelations of his unprinted *Journals* are now to be tested, upon their publication; but they will not decrease or check his growing fame.

SIR WALTER RALEIGH

PERHAPS no one in English history better represents the heroic character than Sir Walter Raleigh, for Sidney has got to be almost as shadowy as Arthur himself. Raleigh's somewhat antique and Roman virtues appear in his numerous military and naval adventures, in his knightly conduct toward the Queen, in his poems and his employments in the Tower, and not least in his death, but more than all in his constant soldier-like bearing and promise. He was the Bayard of peaceful as well as warlike enterprise, and few lives which are the subject of recent and trustworthy history are so agreeable to the imagination. Notwithstanding his temporary unpopularity, he especially possessed the prevalent and popular qualities which command the admiration of men. If an English Plutarch were to be written, Raleigh would be the best Greek or Roman among them all. He was one whose virtues if they were not distinctively great yet gave to virtues a current stamp and value as it were by the very grace and loftiness with which he carried them; — one of nature's noblemen who possessed those requisites to true nobility without which no heraldry nor blood can avail. Among savages he would still have been chief. He seems to have had, not a profounder or grander but, so to speak, *more* nature than other men,—a great, irregular, luxuriant nature, fit to be the darling of a people. The enthusiastic and often extravagant, but always hearty and emphatic, tone in which he is spoken of by his contemporaries is not the least remarkable fact about him, and it does not matter much whether the current stories are true or not, since they at least prove his reputation. It is not his praise to have been a saint or a seer in his generation, but "one of the gallantest worthies that ever England bred." The stories about him testify to a character rather than a virtue. As, for instance, that "he was damnable proud. Old Sir Robert Harley of Brampton-Brian Castle (who knew him) would say, 't was a great question, who was the proudest, Sir Walter or Sir Thomas Overbury, but the difference that was, was judged on Sir Thomas's side;" that "in his youth his companions were boisterous blades, but generally those that had wit;" that on one occasion he beats one of them for making a noise in a tavern, and "seals up his mouth, his upper and nether beard, with hard wax." A young contemporary says, "I have heard his enemies confess that he was one of the weightiest and wisest men that the island ever bred;" and another gives this character of him, — "who hath not known or read of this prodigy of wit and fortune, Sir Walter Raleigh, a man unfortunate in nothing else but in the greatness of his wit and advancement, whose eminent worth was such, both in domestic policy, foreign expeditions, and discoveries, in arts and literature, both practic and contemplative, that it might seem at once to conquer example and imitation."

And what we are told of his personal appearance is accordant with the rest, — that "he had in the outward man a good presence, in a handsome and well-compacted person;" that "he was a tall, handsome, and bold man;" and his "was thought a very good face," though "his countenance was somewhat spoiled by the unusual height of his forehead." "He was such a person (every way), that (as King Charles I says of the Lord Strafford) a prince would rather be afraid of, than ashamed of," and had an "awfulness and ascendency in his aspect over other mortals;" and we are not disappointed to learn that he indulged in a splendid dress, and "notwithstanding his so great mastership in style, and his conversation with the learnedest and politest persons, yet he spake broad Devonshire to his dying day." [1]

Such a character as this was well suited to the time in which he lived. His age was an unusually stirring one. The discovery of America and the successful progress of the Reformation opened a field for both the intellectual and physical energies of his generation. The fathers of his age were Calvin and Knox, and Cranmer, and Pizarro, and Garcilaso; and its immediate forefathers were Luther

[1] All the notes are in the back of the volume.

and Raphael, and Bayard and Angelo, and Ariosto, and Copernicus, and Machiavel, and Erasmus, and Cabot, and Ximenes, and Columbus. Its device might have been an anchor, a sword, and a quill. The Pizarro laid by his sword at intervals and took to his letters. The Columbus set sail for newer worlds still, by voyages which needed not the patronage of princes. The Bayard alighted from his steed to seek adventures no less arduous than heretofore upon the ocean and in the Western world; and the Luther who had reformed religion began now to reform politics and science.

In Raleigh's youth, however it may have concerned him, Camoens was writing a heroic poem in Portugal, and the arts still had their representative in Paul Veronese of Italy. He may have been one to welcome the works of Tasso and Montaigne to England, and when he looked about him he might have found such men as Cervantes and Sidney, men of like pursuits and not altogether dissimilar genius from himself, for his contemporaries, — a Drake to rival him on the sea, and a Hudson in western adventure; a Halley, a Galileo, and a Kepler, for his astronomers; a Bacon, a Behmen, and a Burton, for his philosophers; and a Jonson, a Spenser, and a Shakespeare, his poets for refreshment and inspiration.

But that we may know how worthy he himself was to make one of this illustrious company, and may appreciate the great activity and versatility of his genius, we will glance hastily at the various aspects of his life.

He was a proper knight, a born cavalier, who in the intervals of war betook himself still to the most vigorous arts of peace, though as if diverted from his proper aim. He makes us doubt if there is not some worthier apology for war than has been discovered, for its modes and manners were an instinct with him; and though in his writings he takes frequent occasion sincerely to condemn its folly, and show the better policy and advantage of peace, yet he speaks with the uncertain authority of a warrior still, to whom those juster wars are not simply the dire necessity he would imply.

In whatever he is engaged we seem to see a plume waving over his head, and a sword dangling at his side. Born in 1552, the last year of the reign of Edward VI, we find that not long after, by such instinct as makes the young crab seek the seashore, he has already marched into France, as one of "a troop of a hundred gentlemen volunteers," who are described as "a gallant company, nobly mounted and accoutred, having on their colors the motto, *Finem det mihi virtus* — 'Let valor be my aim.'" And so in fact he marched on through life with this motto in his heart always. All the peace of those days seems to have been but a truce, or casual interruption of the order of war. War with Spain, especially, was so much the rule rather than the exception that the navigators and commanders of these two nations, when abroad, acted on the presumption that their countries were at war at home, though they had left them at peace; and their respective colonies in America carried on war at their convenience, with no infraction of the treaties between the mother countries.

Raleigh seems to have regarded the Spaniards as his natural enemies, and he was not backward to develop this part of his nature. When England was threatened with foreign invasion, the Queen looked to him especially for advice and assistance; and none was better able to give them than he. We cannot but admire the tone in which he speaks of his island, and how it is to be best defended, and the navy, its chief strength, maintained and improved. He speaks from England as his castle, and his (as no other man's) is the voice of the state; for he does not assert the interests of an individual but of a commonwealth, and we see in him revived a Roman patriotism.

His actions, as they were public and for the public, were fit to be publicly rewarded; and we accordingly read with equanimity of gold chains and monopolies and other emoluments conferred on him from time to time for his various services,—his military successes in Ireland, "that commonweal of common woe," as he even then described it; his enterprise in the harbor of Cadiz; his capture of Fayal from the Spaniards; and other exploits which perhaps, more than anything else, got him fame and a name during his lifetime.

If war was his earnest work, it was his pastime too; for in the peaceful intervals we hear of him participating heartily and bearing off the palm in the birthday tournaments and tilting matches of the Queen, where the combatants vied with each other mainly who should come on to the ground in the most splendid dress and equipments. In those tilts it is said that his political rival, Essex, whose wealth enabled him to lead the costliest train, but who ran very ill and was thought the poorest knight of all, was wont to change his suit from orange to green, that it might be said that "There was one in green who ran worse than one in orange."

None of the worthies of that age can be duly appreciated if we neglect to consider them in their relation to the New World. The stirring spirits stood with but one foot on the land. There were Drake, Hawkins, Hudson, Frobisher, and many others, and their worthy companion was Raleigh. As a navigator and naval commander he had few equals, and if the reader who has attended to his other actions inquires how he filled up the odd years, he will find that they were spent in numerous voyages to America for the purposes of discovery and colonization. He would be more famous for these enterprises if they were not overshadowed by the number and variety of his pursuits.

His persevering care and oversight as the patron of Virginia, discovered and planted under his auspices in 1584, present him in an interesting light to the American reader. The work of colonization was well suited to his genius; and if the necessity of England herself had not required his attention and presence at this time, he would possibly have realized some of his dreams in plantations and cities on our coast.

England has since felt the benefit of his experience in naval affairs; for he was one of the first to assert their importance to her, and he exerted himself especially for the improvement of naval architecture, on which he has left a treatise. He also composed a discourse on the art of war at sea, a subject which at that time had never been treated.

We can least bear to consider Raleigh as

a courtier; though the court of England at that time was a field not altogether unworthy of such a courtier. His competitors for fame and favor there were Burleigh, Leicester, Sussex, Buckingham, and, be it remembered, Sir Philip Sidney, whose *Arcadia* was just finished when Raleigh came to court. Sidney was his natural companion and other self, as it were, as if nature, in her anxiety to confer one specimen of a true knight and courtier on that age, had cast two in the same mould, lest one should miscarry. These two kindred spirits are said to have been mutually attracted toward each other. And there, too, was Queen Elizabeth herself, the centre of the court and of the kingdom; to whose service he consecrates himself, not so much as a subject to his sovereign, but as a knight to the service of his mistress. His intercourse with the Queen may well have begun with the incident of the cloak, for such continued to be its character afterward. It has in the description an air of romance, and might fitly have made a part of his friend Sidney's *Arcadia*. The tale runs that the Queen, walking one day in the midst of her courtiers, came to a miry place, when Raleigh, who was then unknown to her, taking off his rich plush cloak, spread it upon the ground for a foot-cloth.

We are inclined to consider him as some knight, and a knight errant, too, who had strayed into the precincts of the court, and practised there the arts which he had learned in bower and hall and in the lists. Not but that he knew how to govern states as well as queens, but he brought to the task the gallantry and graces of chivalry, as well as the judgment and experience of a practical modern Englishman. "The Queen," says one, "began to be taken with his elocution, and loved to hear his reasons to his demands; and the truth is she took him for a kind of oracle, which nettled them all." He rose rapidly in her favor, and became her indispensable counsellor in all matters which concerned the state, for he was minutely acquainted with the affairs of England, and none better understood her commercial interests. But notwithstanding the advantage of his wisdom to England, we had rather think of him taking counsel with the winds and breakers of the American coast and the roar of the Spanish artillery, than with the Queen. But though he made a good use of his influence (for the most part) when obtained, he could descend to the grossest flattery to obtain this, and we could wish him forever banished from the court, whose favors he so earnestly sought. Yet that he who was one while "the Queen of England's poor captive," could sometimes assume a manly and independent tone with her, appears from his answer when she once exclaimed, on his asking a favor for a friend, "When, Sir Walter, will you cease to be a beggar?" "When your gracious Majesty ceases to be a benefactor."

His court life exhibits him in mean and frivolous relations, which make him lose that respect in our eyes which he had acquired elsewhere.

The base use he made of his recovered influence (after having been banished from the court, and even suffered imprisonment in consequence of the Queen's displeasure) to procure the disgrace and finally the execution of his rival Essex (who had been charged with treason) is the foulest stain upon his escutcheon, the one which it is hardest to reconcile with the nobleness and generosity which we are inclined to attribute to such a character. Revenge is most unheroic. His acceptance of bribes afterwards for using his influence in behalf of the earl's adherents is not to be excused by the usage of the times. The times may change, but the laws of integrity and magnanimity are immutable. Nor are the terms on which he was the friend of Cecil, from motives of policy merely, more tolerable to consider. Yet we cannot but think that he frequently travelled a higher, though a parallel, course with the mob, and though he had their suffrages, to some extent deserves the praise which Jonson applies to another, —

> That to the vulgar canst thyself apply,
> Treading a better path not contrary.

We gladly make haste to consider him in what the world calls his misfortune, after the death of Elizabeth and the accession of James I, when his essentially nobler nature was separated from the base company of the court and the contaminations which his loyalty could not resist, though tested by imprisonment and the scaffold.

His enemies had already prejudiced the King against him before James's accession to the throne, and when at length the English nobility were presented to his Majesty (who, it will be remembered, was a Scotchman), and Raleigh's name was told, "Raleigh!" exclaimed the King, "O my soule, mon, I have heard *rawly* of thee." His efforts to limit the King's power of introducing Scots into England contributed to increase his jealousy and dislike, and he was shortly after accused by Lord Cobham of participating in a conspiracy to place the Lady Arabella Stuart[2] on the throne. Owing mainly, it is thought, to the King's resentment, he was tried and falsely convicted of high treason; though his accuser retracted in writing his whole accusation before the conclusion of the trial.

In connection with his earlier behavior to Essex, it should be remembered that by his conduct on his own trial he in a great measure removed the ill-will which existed against him on that account. At his trial, which is said to have been most unjustly and insolently conducted by Sir Edward Coke on the part of the Crown, "he answered," says one, "with that temper, wit, learning, courage, and judgment that, save that it went with the hazard of his life, it was the happiest day that ever he spent." The first two that brought the news of his condemnation to the King were Roger Ashton and a Scotsman, "whereof one affirmed that never any man spake so well in times past, nor would in the world to come; and the other said, that whereas when he saw him first, he was so led with the common hatred that he would have gone a hundred miles to have seen him hanged, he would, ere he parted, have gone a thousand to have saved his life." Another says, "he behaved himself so worthily, so wisely, and so temperately, that in half a day the mind of all the company was changed from the extremest hate to the extremest pity." And another said, "to the lords he was humble, but not prostrate; to the jury affable, but not fawning; to the King's counsel patient, but not yielding to the imputations laid upon him, or neglecting to repel them with the spirit which became an injured and honorable man." And finally he followed the sheriff out of court in the expressive words of Sir Thomas Overbury, "with admirable erection, but yet in such sort as became a man condemned."

Raleigh prepared himself for immediate execution, but after his pretended accomplices had gone through the ceremony of a mock execution and been pardoned by the King, it satisfied the policy of his enemies to retain him a prisoner in the Tower for thirteen years, with the sentence of death still unrevoked. In the meanwhile he solaced himself in his imprisonment with writing a *History of the World* and cultivating poetry and philosophy as the noblest deeds compatible with his confinement.

It is satisfactory to contrast with his mean personal relations while at court his connection in the Tower with the young Prince Henry (whose tastes and aspirations were of a stirring kind), as his friend and instructor.

He addresses some of his shorter pieces to the Prince, and in some instances they seem to have been written expressly for his use. He preaches to him as he was well able, from experience, a wiser philosophy than he had himself practised, and was particularly anxious to correct in him a love of popularity which he had discovered, and to give him useful maxims for his conduct when he should take his father's place.

He lost neither health nor spirits by thirteen years of captivity, but after having spent this, the literary era of his life, as in the retirement of his study, and having written the history of the Old World, he began to dream of actions which would supply materials to the future historian of the New. It is interesting to consider him, a close prisoner as he was, preparing for voyages and adventures which would require him to roam more broadly than was consistent with the comfort or ambition of his freest contemporaries.

Already in 1595, eight years before his imprisonment, it will be remembered he had undertaken his first voyage to Guiana in person; mainly, it is said, to recover favor with the Queen, but doubtless it was much more to recover favor with himself, and exercise his powers in fields more worthy of him than a corrupt court. He continued to cherish this his favorite project though a prisoner; and at length in the thirteenth year of his imprisonment, through the influence of his friends and his confident assertions respecting the utility of the expedition to the country, he obtained his release, and set sail for Guiana with twelve ships. But unfortunately he neglected to procure a formal pardon from the King, trusting to the opinion of Lord Bacon that this was unnecessary, since the sentence of death against him was virtually annulled, by the lives of others being committed to his hands. Acting on this presumption, and with the best intentions toward his country, and only his usual jealousy of Spain, he undertook to make good his engagements to himself and the world.

It is not easy for us at this day to realize what extravagant expectations Europe had formed respecting the wealth of the New

World. We might suppose two whole continents, with their adjacent seas and oceans, equal to the known globe, stretching from pole to pole, and possessing every variety of soil, climate, and productions, lying unexplored to-day, — what would now be the speculations of Broadway and State Street?

The few travellers who had penetrated into the country of Guiana, whither Raleigh was bound, brought back accounts of noble streams flowing through majestic forests, and a depth and luxuriance of soil which made England seem a barren waste in comparison. Its mineral wealth was reported to be as inexhaustible as the cupidity of its discoverers was unbounded. The very surface of the ground was said to be resplendent with gold, and the men went covered with gold-dust, as Hottentots with grease. Raleigh was informed while at Trinidad, by the Spanish governor, who was his prisoner, that one Juan Martinez had at length penetrated into this country; and the stories told by him of the wealth and extent of its cities surpass the narratives of Marco Polo himself. He is said in particular to have reached the city of Manoa, to which he first gave the name of *El Dorado*, or "The Gilded," the Indians conducting him blindfolded, not removing the veil from his eyes till he was ready to enter the city. It was at noon that he passed the gates, and it took him all that day and the next, walking from sunrise to sunset, before he arrived at the palace of Inga, where he resided for seven months, till he had made himself master of the language of the country. These and even more fanciful accounts had Raleigh heard and pondered, both before and after his first visit to the country. No one was more familiar with the stories, both true and fabulous, respecting the discovery and resources of the New World, and none had a better right than he to know what great commanders and navigators had done there, or anywhere. Such information would naturally flow to him of its own accord. That his ardor and faith were hardly cooled by actual observation may be gathered from the tone of his own description.

He was the first Englishman who ascended the Orinoco, and he thus describes the adjacent country: "On the banks were divers sorts of fruits good to eat, besides flowers and trees of that variety as were sufficient to make ten volumes of herbals. We relieved ourselves many times with the fruits of the country, and sometimes with fowl and fish: we saw birds of all colors, some carnation, some crimson, orange tawny, purple, green, watched [watchet], and of all other sorts, both simple and mixt; as it was unto us a great good passing of the time to behold them, besides the relief we found by killing some store of them with our fowling pieces, without which, having little or no bread, and less drink, but only the thick and troubled water of the river, we had been in a very hard case."

The following is his description of the waterfalls and the province of Canuri, through which last the river runs. "When we run to the tops of the first hills of the plains adjoining to the river, we beheld that wonderful breach of waters which ran down Caroli: and might from that mountain see the river how it ran in three parts above twenty miles off; there appeared some ten or twelve overfalls in sight, every one as high over the other as a church tower, which fell with that fury, that the rebound of waters made it seem as if it had been all covered over with a great shower of rain: and in some places we took it at the first for a smoke that had risen over some great town. For mine own part, I was well persuaded from thence to have returned, being a very ill footman; but the rest were all so desirous to go near the said strange thunder of waters, as they drew me on by little and little, into the next valley, where we might better discern the same. I never saw a more beautiful country, nor more lively prospects, hills so raised here and there over the valleys, the river winding into divers branches, the plains adjoining without bush or stubble, all fair green grass, the ground of hard sand, easy to march on either for horse or foot, the deer crossing in every path, the birds towards the evening singing on every tree with a thousand several tunes, cranes and herons of white, crimson, and carnation perching on the river's side, the air fresh, with a gentle easterly wind; and every stone that we stopped to take up promised either gold or silver by his complexion."

In another place he says: "To conclude, Guiana is a country never sacked, turned, nor wrought; the face of the earth hath not been torn, nor the virtue and salt of the soil spent by manurance."

To the fabulous accounts of preceding adventurers Raleigh added many others equally absurd and poetical, as, for instance, of a tribe "with eyes in their shoulders and their mouths in the middle of their breasts," but, it seems to us, with entire good faith, and no such flagrant intent to deceive as he has been accused of. "Weak policy it would be in me," says he, "to betray myself or my country with imaginations; neither am I so far in love with that lodging, watching, care, peril, diseases, ill savors, bad fare, and many other mischiefs that accompany these voyages, as to woo myself again into any of them, were I not assured that the sun covereth not so much riches in any part of the earth." Some portion of this so prevalent delusion respecting the precious metals is no doubt to be referred to the actual presence of an abundance of mica, slate, and talc and other shining substances in the soil. "We may judge," says Macaulay, "of the brilliancy of these deceptious appearances, from learning that the natives ascribed the lustre of the Magellanic clouds or nebulæ of the southern hemisphere to the bright reflections produced by them." So he was himself most fatally deceived, and that too by the strength and candor no less than the weakness of his nature, for, generally speaking, such things are not to be disbelieved as task our imaginations to conceive of, but such rather as are too easily embraced by the understanding.

It is easy to see that he was tempted, not so much by the lustre of the gold, as by the splendor of the enterprise itself. It was the best move that peace allowed. The expeditions to Guiana and the ensuing golden dreams were not wholly unworthy of him, though he accomplished little more in the first voyage than to take formal possession of the country in the name of the Queen, and in the second, of the Spanish town of San Thomé, as his enemies would say, in the name of himself. Perceiving that the Spaniards, who had been secretly informed of his designs through their ambassador in England, were prepared to thwart his endeavors, and resist his progress in the country, he procured the capture of this their principal town, which was also burnt, against his orders.

But it seems that no particular exception is to be taken against these high-handed measures, though his enemies have made the greatest handle of them. His behavior on this occasion was part and parcel of his constant character. It would not be easy to say when he ceased to be an honorable soldier and became a freebooter; nor indeed is it of so much importance to inquire of a man what actions he performed at one and what at another period, as what manner of man he was at all periods. It was after all the same Raleigh who had won so much renown by land and sea, at home and abroad. It was his forte to deal vigorously with men, whether as a statesman, a courtier, a navigator, a planter of colonies, an accused person, a prisoner, an explorer of continents, or a military or naval commander.

And it was a right hero's maxim of his, that "good success admits of no examination;" which, in a liberal sense, is true conduct. That there was no cant in him on the subject of war appears from his saying (which indeed is very true), that "the necessity of war, which among human actions is most lawless, hath some kind of affinity and near resemblance with the necessity of law." It is to be remembered, too, that if the Spaniards found him a restless and uncompromising enemy, the Indians experienced in him a humane and gentle defender, and on his second visit to Guiana remembered his name and welcomed him with enthusiasm.

We are told that the Spanish ambassador, on receiving intelligence of his doings in that country, rushed into the presence of King James, exclaiming "*Piratas, piratas!*" — "Pirates, pirates!" and the King, to gratify his resentment, without bringing him to trial for this alleged new offence, with characteristic meanness and pusillanimity caused him to be executed upon the old sentence soon after his return to England.

The circumstances of his execution and how he bore himself on that memorable occasion, when the sentence of death passed fifteen years before was revived against him, — after as an historian in his confinement he had visited the Old World in his free imagination, and as an unrestrained adventurer the New, with his fleets and in person, — are perhaps too well known to be repeated. The reader will excuse our hasty rehearsal of the final scene.

We can pardon, though not without limitations, his supposed attempt at suicide in the prospect of defeat and disgrace; and no one can read his letter to his wife, written while he was contemplating this act, without being reminded of the Roman Cato, and admiring while he condemns him. "I know," says he, "that it is forbidden to destroy ourselves; but I trust it is forbidden in this sort, that we destroy not ourselves despairing of God's mercy." Though his greatness seems to have forsaken him in his feigning himself sick, and the base methods he took to avoid being brought to trial, yet he recovered himself at last, and happily withstood the trials which awaited him. The night before his execution, besides writing letters of farewell to his wife, containing the most practical advice for the conduct of her life, he appears to have spent the time in writing verses on his condition, and among others this couplet, *On the Snuff of a Candle*.

> Cowards may fear to die; but courage stout,
> Rather than live in snuff, will be put out.

And the following verses, perhaps, for an epitaph on himself:

> Even such is time, that takes on trust
> Our youth, our joys, our all we have,
> And pays us but with earth and dust;
> Who in the dark and silent grave,
> When we have wandered all our ways,
> Shuts up the story of our days!
> But from this earth, this grave, this dust,
> The Lord shall raise me up, I trust!

His execution was appointed on Lord Mayor's day, that the pageants and shows might divert the attention of the people; but those pageants have long since been forgotten, while this tragedy is still remembered. He took a pipe of tobacco before he went to the scaffold, and appeared there with a serene countenance, so that a stranger could not have told which was the condemned person. After exculpating himself in a speech to the people, and without ostentation having felt the edge of the axe, and disposed himself once as he wished to lie, he made a solemn prayer, and being directed to place himself so that his face should look to the east, his characteristic answer was, "It mattered little how the head lay, provided the heart was right." The executioner being overawed was unable at first to perform his office, when Raleigh, slowly raising his head, exclaimed, "Strike away, man, don't be afraid." "He was the most fearless of death," says the bishop [3] who attended him, "that ever was known, and the most resolute and confident, yet with reverence and conscience." But we would not exaggerate the importance of these things. The death scenes of great men are agreeable to consider only when they make another and harmonious chapter of their lives, and we have accompanied our hero thus far because he lived, so to speak, unto the end.

In his *History of the World* occurs this sentence: "O eloquent, just, and mighty Death! Whom none could advise, thou hast persuaded; what none hath dared, thou hast done; and whom all the world hath flattered, thou only hast cast out of the world and despised: thou hast drawn together all the far-stretched greatness, all the pride, cruelty, and ambition of man, and covered it all over with those two narrow words — *Hic iacet!*"

Perhaps Raleigh was the man of the most general information and universal accomplishment of any in England. Though he excelled greatly in but few departments, yet he reached a more valuable mediocrity in many. "He seemed," said Fuller, "to be like Cato Uticensis, born to that only which he was about." He said he had been "a soldier, a sea-captain, and a courtier," but he had been much more than this. He embraced in his studies music, ornamental gardening, painting, history, antiquities, chemistry, and many arts beside. Especially he is said to have been a great chemist, and studied most in his sea voyages, "when he carried always a trunk of books along with him, and had nothing to divert him," and when also he carried his favorite pictures. In the Tower, too, says one, "he doth spend all the day in distillations;" and that this was more than a temporary recreation appears from the testimony of one who says he was operator to him for twelve years. Here also "he conversed on poetry, philosophy, and literature with Hoskins, his fellow-prisoner," whom Ben Jonson mentions as "the person who had polished him." He was a political economist far in advance of his age, and a sagacious and influential speaker in the House of Commons. Science is indebted to him in more ways than one. In the midst of pressing public cares he interested himself to establish some means of universal communication between men of science for their mutual benefit, and actually set up what he termed "An office of address" for this purpose. As a mathematician, he was the friend of Harriot, Dee, and the Earl of Northumberland. As an antiquarian, he was a member of the first antiquarian society established in England, along with Spelman, Selden, Cotton, Camden, Savile, and Stow. He is said to have been the founder of the Mermaid Club, which met in Fleet Street, to which Shakespeare, Ben Jonson, Fletcher, Beaumont, Carew, Donne, etc., belonged. He has the fame of having first introduced the potato from Virginia and the cherry from the Canaries into Ireland, where his garden was; and his manor of Sherborne[4] "he beautified with gardens, and orchards, and groves of much variety and delight." And this fact, evincing his attention to horticulture, is related, that once, on occasion of the Queen's visiting him, he artificially retarded the ripening of some cherries by stretching a wet canvas over the tree, and removed it on a sunny day, so as to present the fruit ripe to the Queen a month later than usual.

Not to omit a more doubtful but not less celebrated benefit, it is said that on the return of his first colonists from Virginia in 1586 tobacco was first effectually introduced into England, and its use encouraged by his influence and example. And finally, not to be outdone by the quacks, he invented a cordial which became very celebrated, bore his name, and was even administered to the Queen, and to the Prince Henry in his last illness. One Febure writes that "Sir Walter, being a worthy successor of Mithridates, Matheolus, Basil Valentine, Paracelsus, and others, has, he affirms, selected all that is choicest in the animal, vegetable, and mineral world, and moreover manifested so much art and experience in the preparation of this great and admirable cordial as will of itself render him immortal."

We come at last to consider him as a literary man and a writer, concerning which aspect of his life we are least indebted to the historian for our facts.

As he was heroic with the sword, so was he with the pen. The *History of the World*, the task which he selected for his prison hours, was heroic in the undertaking and heroic in the achievement. The easy and cheerful heart with which he endured his confinement, turning his prison into a study, a parlor, and a laboratory, and his prison-yard into a garden, so that men did not so much pity as admire him; the steady purpose with which he set about fighting his battles, prosecuting his discoveries, and gathering his laurels, with the pen, if he might no longer with regiments and fleets, — is itself an exploit. In writing the *History of the World* he was indeed at liberty; for he who contemplates truth and universal laws is free, whatever walls immure his body, though to our brave prisoner thus employed, mankind may have seemed but his poor fellow-prisoners still.

Though this remarkable work interests us more, on the whole, as a part of the history of Raleigh than as the *History of the World*, yet it was done like himself, and with no small success. The historian of Greece and Rome is usually unmanned by his subject, as a peasant crouches before lords; but Raleigh, though he succumbs to the imposing fame of tradition and antediluvian story, and exhibits unnecessary reverence for a prophet or patriarch, from his habit of innate religious courtesy, has done better than this whenever a hero was to be dealt with. He stalks down through the aisles of the past, as through the avenues of a camp, with poets and historians for his heralds and guides; and from whatever side the faintest trump reaches his ear, that way does he promptly turn, though to the neglect of many a gaudy pavilion.

From a work so little read in these days we will venture to quote as specimens the following criticisms on Alexander and the character of Epaminondas. They will, at any rate, teach our lips no bad habits. There is a natural emphasis in his style, like a man's tread, and a breathing space between the sentences, which the best of more modern writing does not furnish. His chapters are like English parks, or rather like a Western forest, where the larger growth keeps down the underwood, and one may ride on horseback through the openings.[5]

"Certainly the things that this King did were marvellous, and would hardly have been undertaken by any man else: and though his father had determined to have invaded the lesser Asia, it is like enough that he would have contented himself with some part thereof, and not have discovered the river of Indus, as this man did. The swift course of victory, wherewith he ran over so large a portion of the world, in so short a space, may justly be imputed unto this, that he was never encountered by an equal spirit, concurring with equal power against him. Hereby it came to pass, that his actions, being limited by no greater opposition than desert places, and the mere length of tedious journeys could make, were like the Colossus of Rhodes, not so much to be admired for the workmanship, though therein also praiseworthy, as for the huge bulk. For certainly the things performed by Xenophon, discover as brave a spirit as Alexander's, and working no less exquisitely, though the effects were less material, as were also the forces and power of command, by which it wrought. But he that would find the exact pattern of a noble commander, must look upon such as Epaminondas, that encountering worthy captains, and those better followed than themselves, have by their singular virtue over-topped their valiant enemies, and still prevailed over those that would not have yielded one foot to any other. Such as these are do seldom live to obtain great empires; for it is a work of more labor and longer time to master the equal forces of one hardy and well-ordered state, than to tread down and utterly subdue a multitude of servile nations, compounding the body of a gross unwieldy empire. Wherefore these *parvo potentes*, men that with little have done much upon enemies of like ability, are to be regarded as choice examples of worth; but great conquerors, to be rather admired for the substance of their actions, than the exquisite managing: exactness and greatness concurring so seldom, that I can find no instance of both in one, save only that brave Roman, Cæsar."

Of Epaminondas he says, "So died Epaminondas, the worthiest man that ever was bred in that nation of Greece, and hardly to be matched in any age or country; for he equalled all others in the several virtues, which in each of them were singular. His justice, and sincerity, his temperance, wisdom, and high magnanimity, were no way inferior to his military virtue; in every part whereof he so excelled, that he could not properly be called a wary, a valiant, a politic, a bountiful, or an industrious, and a provident captain; all these titles, and many others being due unto him, which with his notable discipline, and good conduct, made a perfect composition of an heroic general. Neither was his private conversation unanswerable to those high parts, which gave him praise abroad. For he was grave, and yet very affable and courteous; resolute in public business, but in his own particular easy, and of much mildness; a lover of his people, bearing with men's infirmities, witty and pleasant in speech, far from insolence, master of his own affections, and furnished with all qualities that might win and keep love. To these graces were added great ability of body, much eloquence and very deep knowledge of philosophy and learning, wherewith his mind being enlightened, rested not in the sweetness of contemplation, but broke forth into such effects as gave unto Thebes which had ever been an underling, a dreadful reputation among all people adjoining, and the highest command in Greece."

For the most part an author only *writes* history, treating it as a dead subject; but Raleigh *tells* it like a fresh story. A man of action himself, he knew when there was an action coming worthy to be related, and does not disappoint the reader, as is too commonly the case, by recording merely the traditionary admiration or wonder. In commenting upon the military actions of the ancients, he easily and naturally digresses to some perhaps equal action of his own, or within his experience; and he tells how they should have drawn up their fleets or men, with the authority of an admiral or general. The alacrity with which he adverts to some action within his experience, and slides down from the dignified impersonality of the historian into the familiarity and interest of a party and eye-witness, is as attractive as rare. He is often without reproach the Cæsar of his own story. He treats Scipio, Pompey, Hannibal, and the rest quite like equals, and he speaks like an eye-witness, and gives life and reality to the narrative by his very lively understanding and relating of it; especially in those parts in which the mere scholar is most likely to fail. Every reader has observed what a dust the historian commonly raises about the field of battle, to serve as an apology for not making clear the disposition and manœuvring of the parties, so that the clearest idea one gets is of a very vague counteraction or standing over against one another of two forces. In this history we, at least, have faith that these things are right. Our author describes an ancient battle with the vivacity and truth of an eye-witness, and perhaps, in criticising the disposition of the forces, saying they should have stood thus or so, sometimes enforces his assertions in some such style as "I remember being in the harbor of Cadiz," etc., so that, as in Herodotus and Thucydides, we associate the historian with the exploits he describes. But this comes not on account of his fame as a writer, but from the conspicuous part he acted on the world's stage, and his name is of equal mark to us with those of his heroes. So in the present instance, not only his valor as a writer, but the part he acted in his generation, the life of the author, seems fit to make the last chapter in the history he is writing. We expect that when his history is brought to a close it will include his own exploits. However, it is hardly a work to be consulted as authority nowadays, except on the subject of its author's character.

The natural breadth and grasp of the man is seen in the preface itself, which is a sermon with human life for its text. In the first books he discusses with childlike earnestness, and an ingenuity which they little deserved, the absurd and frivolous questions which engaged the theology and philosophy of his day. But even these are recommended by his sincerity and fine imagination, while the subsequent parts, or story itself, have the merit of being far more credible and lifelike than is common. He shows occasionally a poet's imagination, and the innocence and purity of a child (as it were) under a knight's dress, such as were worthy of the friend of Spenser. The nobleness of his nature is everywhere apparent. The gentleness and steady heart with which he cultivates philosophy and poetry in his prison, dissolving in the reader's imagination the very walls and bars by his childlike confidence in truth and his own destiny, are affecting. Even astrology, or, as he has elsewhere called it, "star-learning," comes recommended from his pen, and science will not refuse it.

"And certainly it cannot be doubted," says he, "but the stars are instruments of far greater use, than to give an obscure light, and for men to gaze on after sunset: it being manifest, that the diversity of seasons, the winters and summers, more hot and cold, are not so uncertained by the sun and moon alone, who alway keep one and the same course; but that the stars have also their working therein.

"And if we cannot deny, but that God hath given virtues to springs and fountains, to cold earth, to plants and stones, minerals, and to the excremental parts of the basest living creatures, why should we rob the beautiful stars of their working powers? for seeing they are many in number, and of eminent beauty and magnitude, we may not think, that in the treasury of his wisdom, who is infinite, there can be wanting (even for every star) a peculiar virtue and operation; as every herb, plant, fruit, and flower adorning the face of the earth, hath the like. For as these were not created to beautify the earth alone, and to cover and shadow her dusty face, but otherwise for the use of man and beast, to feed them and cure them; so were not those uncountable glorious bodies set in the firmament, to no other end, than to adorn it; but for instruments and organs of his divine providence, so far as it hath pleased his just will to determine.

"Origen upon this place of *Genesis*, *Let there be light in the firmament, &c.*, affirmeth, that the stars are not causes (meaning perchance binding causes;) but are as open books, wherein are contained and set down all things whatsoever to come; but not to be read by the eyes of human wisdom: which latter part I believe well, and the saying of Syracides withal; *That there are hid yet greater things than these be, and we have seen but a few of his works.* And though, for the capacity of men, we know somewhat, yet in the true and uttermost virtues of herbs and plants, which our selves sow and set, and which grow under our feet, we are in effect ignorant; much more in the powers and working of celestial bodies. . . . But in this question of fate, the middle course is to be followed, that as with the heathen we do not bind God to his creatures, in this supposed necessity of destiny; and so on the contrary we do not rob those beautiful creatures of their powers and offices. . . . And that they wholly direct the reasonless mind, I am resolved: for all those which were created mortal, as birds, beasts, and the like, are left to their natural appetites; over all which, celestial bodies (as instruments and executioners of God's providence) have absolute dominion. . . . And Saint Augustine says, *Deus regit inferiora corpora per superiora*; 'God ruleth the bodies below by those above.' . . . It was therefore truly affirmed, *Sapiens adiuvabit opus astrorum, quemadmodum agricola terrae naturam*; 'A wise man assisteth the work of the stars, as the husbandman helpeth the nature of the soil.' . . . Lastly, we ought all to know, that God created the stars as he did the rest of the universal; whose influences may be called his reserved and unwritten laws. . . . But it was well said of Plotinus, that the stars were significant, but not efficient, giving them yet something less than their due: and therefore as I do not consent with them, who would make those glorious creatures of God virtueless: so I think that we derogate from his eternal and absolute power and providence, to ascribe to them the same dominion over our immortal souls, which they have over all bodily substances, and perishable natures: for the souls of men loving and fearing God, receive influence from that divine light it self, whereof the sun's clarity, and that of the stars, is by Plato called but a shadow, *Lumen est umbra Dei, et Deus est lumen luminis;* 'Light is the shadow of God's brightness, who is the light of light.'"

We are reminded by this of Du Bartas's poem on the *Probability of the Celestial Orbs being inhabited,* translated by Sylvester:[6]

> I 'll ne'er believe that the arch-Architect
> With all these fires the heavenly arches deck'd
> Only for shew, and with their glistering shields
> T' amaze poor shepherds, watching in the fields;

I'll ne'er believe that the least flow'r that pranks
Our garden borders, or the common banks,
And the least stone, that in her warming lap
Our kind nurse Earth doth covetously wrap,
Hath some peculiar virtue of its own,
And that the glorious stars of heav'n have none.

Nor is the following brief review and exaltation of the subject of all history unworthy of a place in this *History of the World:*

"Man, thus compounded and formed by God, was an abstract, or model, or brief story in the universal: . . . for out of the earth and dust was formed the flesh of man, and therefore heavy and lumpish; the bones of his body we may compare to the hard rocks and stones, and therefore strong and durable; of which Ovid:

Inde genus durum sumus experiensque laborum,
Et documenta damus, qua simus origine nati:

From thence our kind hard-hearted is,
  Enduring pain and care,
Approving, that our bodies of
  A stony nature are.

His blood, which disperseth it self by the branches of veins through all the body, may be resembled to those waters, which are carried by brooks and rivers over all the earth ; his breath to the air, his natural heat to the inclosed warmth which the earth hath in it self, which, stirred up by the heat of the sun, assisteth nature in the speedier procreation of those varieties, which the earth bringeth forth ; our radical moisture, oil or balsamum (whereon the natural heat feedeth and is maintained) is resembled to the fat and fertility of the earth ; the hairs of man's body, which adorns, or overshadows it, to the grass, which covereth the upper face and skin of the earth ; our generative power, to nature, which produceth all things ; our determinations, to the light, wandering, and unstable clouds, carried everywhere with uncertain winds ; our eyes to the light of the sun and moon ; and the beauty of our youth, to the flowers of the spring, which, either in a very short time, or with the sun's heat, dry up and wither away, or the fierce puffs of wind blow them from the stalks ; the thoughts of our mind, to the motion of angels ; and our pure understanding (formerly called *mens*, and that which always looketh upwards) to those intellectual natures, which are always present with God; and lastly, our immortal souls (while they are righteous) are by God himself beautified with the title of his own image and similitude."

But man is not in all things like nature: "For this tide of man's life, after it once turneth and declineth, ever runneth with a perpetual ebb and falling stream, but never floweth again, our leaf once fallen, springeth no more; neither doth the sun or the summer adorn us again with the garments of new leaves and flowers."

There is a flowing rhythm in some of these sentences like the rippling of rivers, hardly to be matched in any prose or verse. The following is his poem on the decay of Oracles and Pantheism:

"The fire which the Chaldeans worshipped for a god, is crept into every man's chimney, which the lack of fuel starveth, water quencheth, and want of air suffocateth: Jupiter is no more vexed with Juno's jealousies; death hath persuaded him to chastity, and her to patience; and that time which hath devoured it self, hath also eaten up both the bodies and images of him and his; yea, their stately temples of stone and dureful marble. The houses and sumptuous buildings erected to Baal, can no where be found upon the earth; nor any monument of that glorious temple consecrated to Diana. There are none now in Phoenicia, that lament the death of Adonis; nor any in Libya, Creta, Thessalia, or elsewhere, that can ask counsel or help from Jupiter. The great god Pan hath broken his pipes; Apollo's priests are become speechless; and the trade of riddles in oracles, with the devil's telling men's fortunes therein, is taken up by counterfeit Egyptians, and cozening astrologers."

In his *Discourse of War in General,* (commencing with almost a heroic verse, "The ordinary theme and argument of history is war,") are many things well thought, and many more well said. He thus expands the maxim that corporations have no soul: "But no senate nor civil assembly can be under such natural impulses to honor and justice as single persons. . . . For a majority is nobody when that majority is separated, and a collective body can have no synteresis, or divine ray, which is in the mind of every man, never assenting to evil, but upbraiding and tormenting him when he does it: but the honor and conscience that lies in the majority is too thin and diffusive to be efficacious; for a number can do a great wrong, and call it right, and not one of that majority blush for it. Hence it is, that though a public assembly may lie under great censures, yet each member looks upon himself as little concerned: this must be the reason why a Roman senate should act with less spirit and less honor than any single Roman would do."

He then in the same treatise leaps with easy and almost merry elasticity from the level of his discourse to the heights of his philosophy: "And it is more plain there is not in nature a point of stability to be found; every thing either ascends or declines: when wars are ended abroad, sedition begins at home, and when men are freed from fighting for necessity, they quarrel through ambition."

And he thus concludes this discourse: "We must look a long way back to find the Romans giving laws to nations, and their consuls bringing kings and princes bound in chains to Rome in triumph; to see men go to Greece for wisdom, or Ophir for gold; when now nothing remains but a poor paper remembrance of their former condition.

It would be an unspeakable advantage, both to the public and private, if men would consider that great truth, that no man is wise or safe, but he that is honest. All I have designed is peace to my country; and may England enjoy that blessing when I shall have no more proportion in it than what my ashes make!"

If his philosophy is for the most part poor, yet the conception and expression are rich and generous.

His maxims are not true or impartial, but are conceived with a certain magnanimity which was natural to him, as if a selfish policy could easily afford to give place in him to a more universal and true.

As a fact evincing Raleigh's poetic culture and taste, it is said that, in a visit to the poet Spenser on the banks of the Mulla, which is described in *Colin Clout's Come Home Again*, he anticipated the judgment of posterity with respect to the *Faerie*

Queene, and by his sympathy and advice encouraged the poet to go on with his work, which by the advice of other friends, among whom was Sidney, he had laid aside. His own poems, though insignificant in respect to number and length, and not yet collected into a separate volume, or rarely accredited to Raleigh, deserve the distinct attention of the lover of English poetry, and leave such an impression on the mind that this leaf of his laurels, for the time, well nigh overshadows all the rest.[7] In these few rhymes, as in that country he describes, his life naturally culminates and his secret aspirations appear. They are in some respects more trustworthy testimonials to his character than state papers or tradition; for poetry is a piece of very private history, which unostentatiously lets us into the secret of a man's life, and is to the reader what the eye is to the beholder, the characteristic feature which cannot be distorted or made to deceive. Poetry is always impartial and unbiassed evidence. The whole life of a man may safely be referred to a few deep experiences. When he only sings a more musical line than usual, all his actions have to be retried by a newer and higher standard than before.

The pleasing poem entitled *A Description of the Country's Recreations*,[8] also printed among the poems of Sir Henry Wotton, is well known. The following, which bears evident marks of his pen, we will quote, from its secure and continent rhythm:

FALSE LOVE AND TRUE LOVE

As you came from the holy land
  Of Walsingham,
Met you not with my true love
  By the way as you came?

How shall I know your true love,
  That have met many one,
As I went to the holy land,
  That have come, that have gone.

She is neither white nor brown,
  But as the heavens fair;
There is none hath a form so divine,
  In the earth or the air.

Such a one did I meet, good Sir,
  Such an angelic face;
Who like a queen, like a nymph did appear,
  By her gait, by her grace:

She hath left me here all alone,
  All alone as unknown,
Who sometimes did me lead with herself,
  And me loved as her own:

What 's the cause that she leaves you alone,
  And a new way doth take:
Who loved you once as her own
  And her joy did you make?

I have loved her all my youth,
  But now, old as you see,
Love likes not the falling fruit
  From the withered tree:

Know that Love is a careless child
  And forgets promise past,
He is blind, he is deaf, when he list,
  And in faith never fast:

His desire is a dureless content,
  And a trustless joy;
He is won with a world of despair,
  And is lost with a toy.

Of women-kind such indeed is the love,
  Or the word love abused;
Under which, many childish desires
  And conceits are excused:

But true love is a durable fire
  In the mind ever burning;
Never sick, never old, never dead,
  From itself never turning.

The following will be new to many of our readers:

THE SHEPHERD'S PRAISE OF HIS
SACRED DIANA

Prais'd be Diana's fair and harmless light;
  Prais'd be the dews, wherewith she moists the ground;
Prais'd be her beams, the glory of the night;
  Prais'd be her power, by which all powers abound!

Prais'd be her nymphs, with whom she decks the woods;
  Prais'd be her knights, in whom true honor lives;
Prais'd be that force by which she moves the floods!
  Let that Diana shine, which all these gives!

In heaven, queen she is among the spheres;
  She mistress-like, makes all things to be pure;
Eternity in her oft-change she bears;
  She, Beauty is; by her, the fair endure.

Time wears her not; she doth his chariot guide;
  Mortality below her orb is plac'd;
By her the virtues of the stars down slide;
  In her is Virtue's perfect image cast!

A knowledge pure it is her worth to know:
With *Circes* let them dwell that think not so!

Though we discover in his verses the vices of the courtier, and they are not equally sustained, as if his genius were warped by the frivolous society of the Court, he was capable of rising to unusual heights. His genius seems to have been fitted for short flights of unmatched sweetness and vigor, but by no means for the sustained loftiness of the epic poet. One who read his verses would say that he had not grown to be the man he promised. They have occasionally a strength of character and heroic tone rarely expressed or appreciated; and powers and excellences so peculiar, as to be almost unique specimens of their kind in the language. Those which have reference to his death have been oftenest quoted, and are the best. *The Soul's Errand*[9] deserves to be remembered till her mission is accomplished in the world.

We quote the following, not so well known, with some omissions, from the commencement of—

HIS PILGRIMAGE

Give me my scallop-shell of quiet,
  My staff of faith to walk upon;
My scrip of joy, immortal diet;
  My bottle of salvation;
My gown of glory, (hope's true gage)
And thus I'll take my pilgrimage.

Blood must be my body's balmer,
  No other balm will here be given,
Whilst my soul, like quiet palmer,
  Travels to the land of heaven,
Over all the silver mountains,
Where do spring those nectar fountains:

And I there will sweetly kiss
The happy bowl of peaceful bliss,
Drinking mine eternal fill
Flowing on each milky hill.
My soul will be adry before,
But after, it will thirst no more.

In that happy, blissful day,
  More peaceful pilgrims I shall see,
That have cast off their rags of clay,
  And walk apparell'd fresh like me.

But he wrote his poems, after all, rather with ships and fleets, and regiments of men and horse. At his bidding, navies took their place in the channel, and even from prison he fitted out fleets with which to realize his golden dreams, and invited his companions to fresh adventures.

Raleigh might well be studied if only for the excellence of his style, for he is remarkable even in the midst of so many masters. All the distinguished writers of that period possess a greater vigor and naturalness than the more modern, and when we read a quotation from one of them in the midst of a modern authority, we seem to have come suddenly upon a greener ground and greater depth and strength of soil. It is as if a green bough were laid across the page, and we are refreshed as if by the sight of fresh grass in midwinter or early spring. You have constantly the warrant of life and experience in all you read. The little that is said is supplied by implication of the much that was done. The sentences are verdurous and blooming as evergreen and flowers, because they are rooted in fact and experience; but our false and florid sentences have only the tints of flowers without their sap or roots. Where shall we look for standard English but to the words of a standard man? The word which is best said came very near not being spoken at all; for it is cousin to a deed which would have been better done. It must have taken the place of a deed by some urgent necessity, even by some misfortune, so that the truest writer will be some captive knight after all.

And perhaps the fates had such a design, when, having stored Raleigh so richly with the substance of life and experience, they made him a fast prisoner, and compelled him to make his words his deeds, and transfer to his expression the emphasis and sincerity of his action.

The necessity of labor, and conversation with many men and things, to the scholar, is rarely well remembered. Steady labor with the hands, which engrosses the attention also, is the best method of removing palaver out of one's style both of talking and writing. If he has worked hard from morning till night, though he may have grieved that he could not be watching the train of his thoughts during that time, yet the few hasty lines which at evening record his day's experience will be more musical and true, than his freest but idle fancy could have furnished. He will not lightly dance at his work who has wood to cut and cord before nightfall in the short days of winter, but every stroke will be husbanded and ring soberly through the wood; [10] and so will the stroke of that scholar's pen, when at evening this records the story of the day, ring soberly on the ear of the reader long after the echoes of his axe have died away. The scholar may be sure he writes the tougher truths for the calluses on his palms. They give firmness to the sentence. We are often astonished at the force and precision of style to which hard-working men unpractised in writing easily attain, when required to make the effort; as if sincerity and plainness, those ornaments of style, were better taught on the farm or in the workshop than in the schools. The sentences written by such rude hands are nervous and tough, like hardened thongs, the sinews of the deer, or the roots of the pine. The scholar might frequently emulate the propriety and emphasis of the farmer's call to his team, and confess, if that were written, it would surpass his *labored* sentences.

From the weak and flimsy periods of the politician and literary man we are glad to turn even to the description of work, the simple record of the month's labor in the farmer's almanac, to restore our tone and spirits. We like that a sentence should read as if its author, had he held a plough instead of a pen, could have drawn a furrow deep and straight to the end. The scholar requires hard labor to give an impetus to his thought; he will learn to grasp the pen firmly so, and wield it gracefully and effectually as an axe or sword. When we consider the weak and nerveless periods of some literary men, who perchance in feet and inches come up to the standard of their race, and are not deficient in girth also, we are amazed at the immense sacrifice of thews and sinews. What! these proportions, these bones, and this their work! Hands which could have felled an ox have hewed this fragile matter which would not have tasked a lady's fingers. Can this be a stalwart man's work, who has a marrow in his back and a tendon Achilles in his heel? They who set up Stonehenge did somewhat, if they only laid out their strength for once, and stretched themselves.

Yet after all the truly efficient laborer will be found not to crowd his day with work, but will saunter to his task, surrounded by a wide halo of ease and leisure, and then do but what he likes best. He is anxious only about the kernels of time. Though the hen should set all day she could lay only one egg, and besides, she would not have picked up the materials for another.

A perfectly healthy sentence is extremely rare. But for the most part we miss the hue and fragrance of the thought. As if we could be satisfied with the dews of the morning or evening without their colors, or the heavens without their azure. The most attractive sentences are perhaps not the wisest, but the surest and soundest. They are spoken firmly and conclusively, as if the author had a right to know what he says; and if not wise, they have at least been well learned. At least he does not stand on a rolling stone, but is well assured of his footing; and if you dispute their doctrine, you will yet allow that there is truth in their assurance. Raleigh's are of this sort, spoken with entire satisfaction and heartiness. They are not so much philosophy as poetry. With him it was always well done and nobly said. His learning was in his hand, and he carried it by him and used it as adroitly as his sword. Aubrey says, "He was no slug; without doubt had a wonderful waking spirit, and great judgment to guide it." He wields his pen as one who sits at ease in his chair, and has a healthy and able body to back his wits, and not a torpid and diseased one to fetter them. In whichever hand is the pen we are sure there is a sword in the other. He sits with his armor on, and with one ear open to hear if the trumpet sound, as one who has stolen a little leisure from the duties of a camp; and we are confident that the whole man, as real and palpable as an Englishman can be, sat down to the writing of his books, and not some curious brain only. Such a man's mere daily exercise in literature might well attract us, and Cecil has said, "He can toil terribly."

Raleigh seems to have been too genial and loyal a soul to resist the temptations of a court; but if to his genius and culture could have been added the temperament of George Fox or Oliver Cromwell, perhaps the world would have had reason longer to remember him. He was, however, the most generous nature that could be drawn into the precincts of a court, and carried the courtier's life almost to the highest pitch of magnanimity and grace of which it was capable. He was liberal and generous as a prince, that is, within bounds; brave, chivalrous, heroic, as a knight in armor —but not as a defenceless man. His was not the heroism of a Luther, but of a Bayard, and had more of grace than of honest truth in it. He had more taste than appetite. There may be something petty in a refined taste,— it easily degenerates into effeminacy. It does not consider the broadest use, and is not content with simple good and bad, but is often fastidious, and curious, or nice only.

His faults, as we have hinted before, were those of a courtier and a soldier. In his counsels and aphorisms we see not unfrequently the haste and rashness of the soldier, strangely mingled with the wisdom of the philosopher. Though his philosophy was not wide nor profound, it was continually giving way to the generosity of his nature, and he was not hard to be won to the right.

What he touches he adorns by a greater humanity and native nobleness, but he touches not the truest nor deepest. He does not in any sense unfold the new, but embellishes the old, and with all his promise of originality he never was quite original, or steered his own course. He was of so fair and susceptible a nature, rather than broad or deep, that he delayed to slake his thirst at the nearest and most turbid wells of truth and beauty; and his homage to the least fair and noble left no room for homage to the All-fair. The misfortune and incongruity of the man appear in the fact that he was at once the author of the *Maxims of State* and *The Soul's Errand*.

When we reconsider what we have said in the foregoing pages, we hesitate to apply any of their eulogy to the actual and historical Raleigh, or any of their condemnation to that ideal Raleigh which he suggests. For we must know the man of history as we know our contemporaries, not so much by his deeds, which often belie his real character, as by the expectation he begets in us — and there is a bloom and halo about the character of Raleigh which defies a close and literal scrutiny, and robs us of our critical acumen. With all his heroism, he was not heroic enough ; with all his manliness, he was servile and dependent; with all his aspirations, he was ambitious. He was not upright nor constant, yet we would have trusted him; he could flatter and cringe, yet we should have respected him; and he could accept a bribe, yet we should confidently have appealed to his generosity.

Such a life is useful for us to contemplate as suggesting that a man is not to be measured by the virtue of his described actions, or the wisdom of his expressed thoughts merely, but by that free character he is, and is felt to be, under all circumstances. Even talent is respectable only when it indicates a depth of character unfathomed. Surely it is better that our wisdom appear in the constant success of our spirits than in our business, or the maxims which fall from our lips merely. We want not only a revelation, but a nature behind to sustain it. Many silent, as well as famous, lives have been the result of no mean thought, though it was never adequately expressed nor conceived; and perhaps the most illiterate and unphilosophical mind may yet be accustomed to think to the extent of the noblest action. We all know those in our own circle who do injustice to their entire character in their conversation and in writing, but who, if actually set over against us, would not fail to make a wiser impression than many a wise thinker and speaker.

We are not a little profited by any life which teaches us not to despair of the race; and such effect has the steady and cheerful bravery of Raleigh. To march sturdily through life, patiently and resolutely looking grim defiance at one's foes, that is one way; but we cannot help being more attracted by that kind of heroism which relaxes its brows in the presence of danger, and does not need to maintain itself strictly, but, by a kind of sympathy with the universe, generously adorns the scene and the occasion, and loves valor so well that itself would be the defeated party only to behold it; which is as serene and as well pleased with the issue as the heavens which look down upon the field of battle. It is but a lower height of heroism when the hero wears a sour face. We fear that much of the heroism which we praise nowadays is dyspeptic. When we consider the vast Xerxean army of reformers in these days, we cannot doubt that many a grim soul goes silent, the hero of some small intestine war; and it is somewhat to begin to live on corn-bread solely, for one who has before lived on bolted wheat; — but of this sort surely are not the deeds to be sung. These are not the Arthurs that inflame the imaginations of men. All fair action is the product of enthusiasm, and nature herself does nothing in the prose mood, though sometimes grimly with poetic fury, and at others humorously. There is enthusiasm in the sunrise and the summer, and we imagine that the shells on the shore take new layers from year to year with such rapture as the bard writes his poems.

We would fain witness a heroism which is literally illustrious, whose daily life is the stuff of which our dreams are made; so that the world shall regard less what it does than how it does it; and its actions unsettle the common standards, and have a right to be done, however wrong they may be to the moralist.

Mere gross health and cheerfulness are no slight attraction, and some biographies have this charm mainly. For the most part the best man's spirit makes a fearful sprite to haunt his grave, and it adds not a little therefore to the credit of Little John, the celebrated follower of Robin Hood, reflecting favorably on the character of his life, that his grave was "long celebrous for the yielding of excellent whetstones."

A great cheerfulness indeed have all great wits and heroes possessed, almost a profane levity to such as understood them not, but their religion had the broader basis of health and permanence. For the hero, too, has his religion, though it is the very opposite to that of the ascetic. It demands not a narrower cell but a wider world. He is perhaps the very best man of the world; the poet active, the saint wilful; not the most godlike, but the most manlike. There have been souls of a heroic stamp for whom this world seemed expressly made; as if this fair creation had at last succeeded, for it seems to be thrown away on the saint. Such seem to be an essential part of their age if we consider them in time, and of the scenery if we consider them in Nature. They lie out before us ill-defined and uncertain, like some scraggy hillside or pasture, which varies from day to day and from hour to hour, with the revolutions of Nature, so that the eye of the forester never rests twice upon the same scene; one knows not what may occur, — he may hear a fox bark or a partridge drum. They are planted deep in Nature and have more root than others. They are earth-born (γηγενεῖς), as was said of the Titans. They are brothers of the sun and moon, they belong, so to speak, to the natural family of man. Their breath is a kind of wind, their step like that of a quadruped, their moods the seasons, and they are as serene as Nature. Their eyes are deep-set like moles or glow-worms, they move free and unconstrained through Nature as her guests, their motions easy and natural as if their course were already determined for them; — as of rivers flowing through valleys, not as somewhat finding a place in Nature, but for whom a place is already found. We love to hear them speak though we do not hear what they say. The very air seems forward to modulate itself into speech for them, and their words are of its own substance, and fall naturally on the ear, like the rustling of leaves and the crackling of the fire. They have the heavens for their abettors, for they never stood from under them, and they look at the stars with an answering ray. The distinctions of better and best, sense and nonsense, seem trivial and petty, when such great healthy indifferences come along. We lay aside the trick of thinking well to attend to their thoughtless and happy natures, and are inclined to show a divine politeness and heavenly good-breeding, for they compel it. They are great natures. It takes a good deal to support them. Theirs is no thin diet. The very air they breathe seems rich, and, as it were, perfumed.

They are so remarkable as to be least remarked at first, since they are most in harmony with the time and place, and if we wonder at all it will be at ourselves and not at them. Mountains do not rise perpendicularly, but the lower eminences hide the higher, and we at last reach their top by a gentle acclivity. We must abide a long time in their midst and at their base, as we spend many days at the Notch of the White Mountains in order to be impressed by the scenery. Let us not think that Alexander will conquer Asia the first time we are introduced to him, though smaller men may be in haste to re-enact their exploits then.

"Would you have
Such an Herculean actor in the scene,
And not his hydra?"
"They must sweat no less
To fit their properties than to express their parts."

The presence of heroic souls enhances the beauty and ampleness of Nature herself. Where they walk, as Vergil says of the abodes of the blessed, —

Largior hic campos aether et lumine vestit
Purpureo: solemque suum, sua sidera norunt.

Here a more copious air invests the fields, and clothes with purple light; and they know their own sun and their own stars.[11]

But, alas! What is Truth? That which we know not. What is Beauty? That which we see not. What is Heroism? That which we are not. It is in vain to hang out flags on a day of rejoicing, — fresh bunting, bright and whole; better the soiled and torn remnant which has been borne in the wars.

We have considered a fair specimen of an Englishman in the sixteenth century; but it behoves us to be fairer specimens of American men in the nineteenth. The gods have given man no constant gift, but the power and liberty to act greatly. How many wait for health and warm weather to be heroic and noble! We are apt to think there is a kind of virtue which need not be heroic and brave, — but in fact virtue is the deed of the bravest; and only the hardy souls venture upon it, for it deals in what we have no experience, and alone does the rude pioneer work of the world. In winter is its campaign, and it never goes into quarters. "Sit not down," said Sir Thomas Browne, "in the popular seats and common level of virtues, but endeavor to make them heroical. Offer not only peace-offerings, but holocausts, unto God."

In our lonely chambers at night we are thrilled by some far-off serenade within the mind, and seem to hear the clarion sound and clang of corselet and buckler from many a silent hamlet of the soul, though actually it may be but the rattling of some farmer's waggon rolling to market against the morrow.[12]

NOTES

From the first tentative draft of the MS. of Thoreau's *Sir Walter Raleigh*

1. Another and kindred spirit contemporary with Raleigh, who survives yet more exclusively in his reputation, rather than in his works, and has been the subject perhaps of even more and more indiscriminate praise, is Sir Philip Sidney; a man who was no less a presence to his contemporaries, though we now look in vain in his works for satisfactory traces of his greatness. Who, dying at the age of thirty-two, having left no great work behind him, or the fame of a single illustrious exploit, has yet left the rumor of a character for heroic impulses and gentle behavior which bids fair to survive the longer lives and more illustrious deeds of many a worthy else, the splendor of whose reputation seems to have blinded his critics to the faults of his writings. So that we find his *Arcadia* spoken of with vague and dubious praise as "a book most famous for rich conceits and splendor of courtly expressions." With regard to whom also this reason is assigned why no monument should be erected to him,

that "he is his own monument whose memory is eternized in his writings, and who was born into the world to show unto our age a sample of ancient virtue," and of whom another says, "It was he whom Queen Elizabeth called her Philip; the Prince of Orange, his master; and whose friendship my Lord Brook was so proud of, that he would have no other epitaph on his grave than this:

'Here lieth Sir Philip Sidney's Friend.'"

From *Raleigh*, by Edmund Gosse

2. Arabella Stuart (born about 1575) was James I's first cousin, the daughter of Charles Stuart, fifth Earl of Lennox, Lord Darnley's elder brother. About 1588 she had come up to London to be presented to Elizabeth, and on that occasion had amused Raleigh with her gay accomplishments. The legal quibble on which her claim was founded was the fact that she was born in England, whereas James as a Scotchman was supposed to be excluded. Arabella was no pretender; her descent from Margaret, the sister of Henry VIII, was complete, and if James had died childless, and she had survived him, it is difficult to see how her claim could have been avoided in favor of the Suffolk line.

3. Dr. Robert Tounson, then Dean of Westminster, who became Bishop of Salisbury. [Gosse.]

4. There is a pleasant legend that Raleigh and one of his half-brothers were riding up to town from Plymouth, when Raleigh's horse stumbled and threw him within the precincts of a beautiful Dorsetshire estate, then in possession of the Dean and Chapter of Salisbury, and that Raleigh, choosing to consider that he had thus taken seisin of the soil, asked the Queen for Sherborne[1] Castle when he arrived at Court. It may have been on this occasion that Elizabeth asked him when he would cease to be a beggar, and received the reply, "When your Majesty ceases to be a benefactor." [GOSSE.]

5. This passage about Alexander and Epaminondas is preceded in Ralegh, as copied by Thoreau in the scrap-book, by some general remarks on that remarkable quality in a few men which Ralegh seems to have felt in himself, which, as he wrote, "Guided handfuls of men against multitudes of equal bodily strength, contrived victories beyond all hope and discourse of reason, converted the fearful passions of his own followers into magnanimity, and the valor of his enemies into cowardice. Such spirits have been stirred up in sundry ages of the world, and in divers parts thereof, to erect and cast down again, to establish and to destroy, and to bring all things, persons and states to the same certain ends which the infinite Spirit

[1] Sherborne came into Ralegh's possession in 1592. — ED.

of the Universal, piercing, moving and governing all things, hath ordained." It was passages like this, in his speech and writings, that laid Ralegh open to the charge of atheism, which seems to have been first brought against him at the same time that his friend the poet Marlowe was similarly accused, in 1592–3, and may have been one of the reasons why Queen Elizabeth withdrew her favor from Ralegh about that time. The definite accusations against Marlowe, which were sent to Queen Elizabeth in June, 1592, apparently, were from the mouth of one Richard Baine, who was hanged for felony two years after, and contained these words, perhaps pointing towards Ralegh: "That one Richard Cholmelei hath confessed that he was persuaded by Marlowe's reason to become an atheist. These things shall by good and honest men be proved to be his opinions and common speeches, and that this Marlowe doth not only hold them himself, but almost in every company he cometh, persuadeth men to atheism, — willing them not to be afraid of bugbears and hobgoblins, and utterly scorning both God and his ministers. . . . He saith, moreover, that he hath quoted a number of contrarieties out of the Scriptures, which he hath given to some great men, who in convenient time shall be named." That Ralegh was one of these "great men" is highly probable; at any rate, the accusation of atheism was then secretly brought against him, and was likely to have weighed with

Elizabeth. Ralegh, with Sidney, is believed to have been one of the English circle who associated with Giordano Bruno, during his short residence in England, a few years before Sidney's death; and Bruno also made himself liable to a like charge of atheism. [F. B. SANBORN.]

6. These lines appear in *The Fourth Day of the First Week* of Sylvester's version of Guillaume Salluste du Bartas's *Divine Weeks and Works*, pp. 102–3 of the edition of 1613. Sylvester adds, at the end of those quoted, continuing the sentence, —

> But shine in vain, and have no charge precise
> But to be walking in Heaven's galleries,
> And through that Palace up and down to clamber
> As Golden Gulls about a Prince's Chamber.

This conceit of the influence of the stars was general in Ralegh's day. His friend Sidney, in his Sonnet XXVI, has the same thought as Ralegh, but turns it to a compliment to Stella, —

> Though dusty wits dare scorn Astrology,
>   And (fools) can think those lamps of purest light
> Whose numbers, way, greatness, eternity,
>   Promising wonders, wonder do invite,
> To have for no cause birthright in the sky,
>   But for to spangle the black weeds of Night;
> Or for some brawl, which in that chamber high
>   They should still dance, to please a gazer's sight.

For me, I do Nature unidle know,
And know great causes great effects procure,
And know, those bodies high rule o'er the low;
And if these rules did fail, proof makes me sure, —
Who oft forejudge my after-following race
By only those two stars in Stella's face.

In what follows, concerning the powers and bodily nature of man, Ralegh uses what was a commonplace of his period, but expresses this quaint conceit with more grace than was customary, and closes it with that touch of regret so familiar in him, though in expression he may borrow from the Sicilian lament of Moschus for Bion. And so poetical is his prose at times, that Thoreau very properly calls the passage on the decay of oracles a "poem." [F. B. SANBORN.]

From Thoreau's second draft of the MS.

7. Aubrey says, "I well remember his study [at Durham-house] which was on a little turret that looked into and over the Thames, and had the prospect, which is as pleasant, perhaps, as any in the world, and which not only refreshes the eie-sight, but cheers the spirits, and (to speake my mind) I believe enlarges an ingeniose man's thoughts." Perhaps it was here that he composed some of his poems.

8. A DESCRIPTION OF THE COUNTRY'S RECREATIONS

Quivering fears, heart-tearing cares,
Anxious sighs, untimely tears,
    Fly, fly to courts;
    Fly to fond worldlings' sports,
Where strain'd sardonic smiles are glosing still,
And grief is forc'd to laugh against her will;
    Where mirth's but mummery;
    And sorrows only real be!

Fly from our country pastimes! fly,
Sad troop of human misery;
    Come, serene looks,
    Clear as the crystal brooks,
Or the pure azur'd heaven, that smiles to see
The rich attendance of our poverty.
    Peace, and a secure mind,
    Which all men seek, we only find.

Abused mortals! did you know
Where joy, heart's-ease, and comforts grow,
    You'd scorn proud towers,
    And seek them in these bowers,
Where winds sometimes our woods perhaps may shake,
But blustering care could never tempest make;
    Nor murmurs e'er come nigh us,
    Saving of fountains that glide by us.

Here's no fantastic masque, nor dance,
But of our kids, that frisk and prance:
    Nor wars are seen,
    Unless upon the green

Two harmless lambs are butting one the other,
Which done, both bleating run, each to his mother;
And wounds are never found,
Save what the plough-share gives the ground.

Here are no false entrapping baits,
To hasten too too hasty fates;
Unless it be
The fond credulity
Of silly fish, which, worldling-like, still look
Upon the bait, but never on the hook:
Nor envy, unless among
The birds, for prize of their sweet song.

Go! let the diving negro seek
For gems hid in some forlorn creek;
We all pearls scorn,
Save what the dewy morn
Congeals upon each little spire of grass,
Which careless shepherds beat down as they pass;
And gold ne'er here appears,
Save what the yellow Ceres bears.

Blest, silent groves! O may ye be
For ever mirth's best nursery!
May pure contents
For ever pitch their tents
Upon these downs, these meads, these rocks, these moun-
tains,
And peace still slumber by these purling fountains!
Which we may every year
Find when we come a fishing here!

9. THE SOUL'S ERRAND[1]

Go, soul, the body's guest,
  Upon a thankless errand;
Fear not to touch the best
  The truth shall be thy warrant
    Go, since I needs must die,
    And give them all the lie.

Go, tell the court it glows,
  And shines like painted wood;
Go, tell the church it shews
  What's good, but does no good.
    If court and church reply,
    Give court and church the lie.

Tell potentates, they live
  Acting, but O their actions!
Not lov'd, unless they give;
  Nor strong, but by their factions.
    If potentates reply,
    Give potentates the lie.

[1] This poem (also called *The Lie* and *The Farewell*) has been given as written by Sir Walter Ralegh, *the night before his execution*, which was October 29, 1618; but it had already appeared in Davison's *Rhapsody*, in 1608; and it is also to be found in a MS. collection of Poems in the British Museum, which has the date of 1596. With the title, *The Lie*, it is printed by Davison with many variations, e. g., —

Say to the court it glows,
  And shines like rotten wood, &c., &c. — ED.

Tell men of high condition,
That rule affairs of state,
Their purpose is ambition;
Their practice only hate.
And if they do reply,
Then give them all the lie.

Tell those that brave it most,
They beg for more by spending;
Who in their greatest cost
Seek nothing but commending.
And if they make reply,
Spare not to give the lie.

Tell zeal it lacks devotion;
Tell love it is but lust;
Tell time it is but motion;
Tell flesh it is but dust:
And wish them not reply,
For thou must give the lie.

Tell age it daily wasteth;
Tell honor how it alters;
Tell beauty that it blasteth;
Tell favor that she falters:
And as they do reply,
Give every one the lie.

Tell wit how much it wrangles
In fickle points of niceness;
Tell wisdom she entangles
Herself in over-wiseness:
And if they do reply,
Then give them both the lie.

Tell physic of her boldness;
  Tell skill it is pretension;
Tell charity of coldness;
  Tell law it is contention:
    And if they yield reply,
    Then give them still the lie.

Tell fortune of her blindness;
  Tell nature of decay;
Tell friendship of unkindness;
  Tell justice of delay:
    And if they do reply,
    Then give them all the lie.

Tell arts they have no soundness,
  But vary by esteeming;
Tell schools they lack profoundness,
  And stand too much on seeming.
    If arts and schools reply,
    Give arts and schools the lie.

Tell faith it's fled the city;
  Tell how the country erreth;
Tell manhood, shakes off pity;
  Tell virtue, least preferreth.
    And if they do reply,
    Spare not to give the lie.

So, when thou hast, as I
  Commanded thee, done blabbing;
Although to give the lie
  Deserves no less than stabbing
    Yet stab at thee who will,
    No stab the soul can kill.

10. The allusion here is doubtless to Thoreau's intimate companion of forty years from early in 1843, Ellery Channing, who in the winter of 1843–44 was chopping cordwood on the road from Concord to Lincoln, near where Thoreau and his friend, Stearns Wheeler of Lincoln, had a cabin in the woods for study and amusement. Channing's experiences that winter gave occasion to the making of a poem, *The Woodman*, which gave title to his third book of verses, published in 1849 (the year when *The Week* came out) and was reprinted in 1902, with omissions and additions, from the Channing MSS. in *Poems of Sixty-Five Years*. Thoreau himself had sometimes been a wood-cutter; indeed, his range of manual employments, as he wrote his Harvard Class Secretary in 1847, made him "a Surveyor, a Gardener, a Farmer, a Painter (I mean a House-painter), a Carpenter, a Mason, a Day-laborer, a Pencil-maker, a etc."

In a letter to Horace Greeley, of May, 1848, Thoreau said that he had supported himself by manual labor at a dollar a day for the past five years, and yet had seen more leisure than most scholars found. He added, "There is no reason why the scholar, who professes to be a little wiser than the mass of men, should not do his work in the dirt occasionally, and by means of his superior wisdom make much less suffice for him. A wise man will not be unfortunate, — how then would you know but he was a fool?"

His friend Emerson, however, did not find that the laborer's strokes that he used himself in his "pleached garden" helped him to better strokes of the pen; and so employed Alcott, Channing, and Thoreau now and then to make the laborer's strokes for him, while he meditated in his study or walked the woods and fields. [F. B. SANBORN.]

11. This trait of cheerfulness was Thoreau's own, and should be named in all mention of him, especially in the long endurance of his last illness. It is well known that the son and namesake of Horace Mann was the companion of Thoreau on that long journey to the unsettled parts of Minnesota in 1861, from which he returned only to linger and die in May, 1862. Mrs. Mann, the mother of young Horace (who himself did not long survive), thus wrote in May of that year to her sister, Mrs. Hawthorne: "I was màde very happy to-day by seeing Miss Thoreau, whose brother died such a happy, peaceful death, — leaving them all so fully possessed of his faith in the Immortal Life that they seem almost to have entered it with him. They said [meaning Mrs. Thoreau, her sister, Louisa Dunbar, and his other aunts, as well as Sophia, his sister], they never could be sad in his presence for a moment; he had been the happiest person they had ever known, all through his life, and was just as happy in the presence of death. This is the more remarkable, as he was still in the prime of life, with a vivid sense of its enjoyments. But he was nearer to the heart of Nature than most men. Sophia said to-day that he once told her when looking at a pressed flower that he had walked 10,000 miles to verify the day on which that flower bloomed. It grew four miles from his home, and he walked there every day in the season of it for many years. . . . He seemed to walk straight into Heaven. It is animating and inspiring to see a great or a good man take that last step with his thoughts about him, and intent upon the two worlds whose connection he sees with the clairvoyance that death gives. I know it well, and I could fully sympathize in her sense of her brother's continued presence. Death is not the word to use for such a transit, — but more life, — for which we as yet have no word."

In a letter to Thoreau's good friend at New Bedford, Daniel Ricketson (printed in Anna and Walton Ricketson's Memoir of their father, p. 142), Sophia, under date of May 20, 1862, said: "During Henry's long illness I never heard a murmur escape him, or the slightest wish expressed to remain with us; his perfect contentment was truly wonderful. None of his friends seemed to realize how very ill he was, so full of life and good cheer did he seem. One friend, as if by way of consolation, said to him, 'Well, Mr. Thoreau, we must all go.' Henry replied, 'When I was a very little boy I learned that I must die, and I set that down, — so of course I am not disappointed now. Death is as near to you as it is to me.' . . . The devotion of his friends was most rare and touching. He would sometimes say 'I should be ashamed to stay in this world after so much had been done for me; I could never repay my friends.'"

In this last sally of his wit, which was as marked in its expression during his illness as in his vigorous days of rambling and writing, we see not alone the humor, but likewise that strict sense of obligation which he had from boyhood. He wished to receive nothing gratis except from Nature herself; his debts, unlike those of many poets, must always be punctually paid. [F. B. SANBORN.]

12. In this description of Virtue, Thoreau made some use of the MS. afterward printed in Mr. Sanborn's edition, in which he quoted the same passage from Sir Thomas Browne, but without giving the author's name. A portion of the illustration of the clarion and corselet is also found in *The Service*. That this whole Ralegh sketch was given as a winter lecture in the Concord Lyceum is rendered probable by his speaking here of "waiting for warm weather," and of a winter campaign. If the records of that Lyceum were complete we might find the very evening on which he read it there,—not later, I am sure, than 1845. [F. B. Sanborn.]

Printed in Great Britain
by Amazon